Arrant Press

❦

The Crime of Rhyme

Happy Hour   *Tom Conyers 2001*

Tom Conyers, an award-winning filmmaker (The Caretaker –
2012), is also a playwright, painter, illustrator and photographer.
To check out his other work, including the novels *One Shot,
Forever Human* and *Morse Code for Cats*, please visit his website:

www.tomconyers.com

THE CRIME OF RHYME

Published by Arrant Press

P.O. Box 406

Burwood, Australia - 3125

Edited by Professor Robert Conyers

Cover Design & Typesetting by Darko Kuzmanović

Cover & Interior Illustrations by Tom Conyers

ISBN-10: 0980587123
ISBN-13: 978-0980587128 (Arrant Press)

The Crime of Rhyme

Tom Conyers

Arrant
Press

Author's Preface

Many of the poems and drawings in this collection date from my
school days. Family and friends have long known of their existence but
few have seen more than a handful. These same people have
encouraged me to exhibit the poems and drawings as a whole. Giving
in to these requests, I handed them over to the most persistent
among them, my father, who assured me they attest to the felicities of
youth, and as such might not be without interest to the general
reader.

He has culled, edited and sorted them into the present layout
discarding the later poetry and drawings as belonging to a different
mindset. He was careful to marry the various styles of drawing with
the different moods of poetry. Therefore, think of the drawings not so
much as illustrations, which they cannot rightly be called, but more as
visual mates partnered, hopefully in comfortable union, to the verse. I
view this book as my written and pictorial certificate of completion for
the trying test of young adulthood. In short, a reliquary for youth.

Tom Conyers, Melbourne 2014

CONTENTS

QUIDDITY

MORTALITY

FANCY

GRAVITY

WHIMSY

PROSPECT

QUIDDITY

Viability

Essence

Vitality

Entity

Life

Life

The other night I dreamt a dream,
　A dream I dreamt the other night,
In which the Snake did rule supreme,
　Supremely ruled, from left to right.
From left to right in checkers were
　A country's lands arrayed by Snake,
Wherein the game would oft recur
　Where I would duly undertake
To climb the ladders ranged about,
　And reach this country's very top,
But I would just as often slip
　Upon a snake and drop,
Until the game had made me mad
　(– Some say even madder –),
And then it came my turn to be
　Stepped on, like a ladder.

Conversation

Much of what is said is soon forgotten.
The rest, no sooner said, goes quickly rotten.

Alice

Alice is always smiling,
So belief in her is hard.
When she is not near
She will thin out and disappear.
I look at her and slightly start,
Squeeze her shoulder hard,
And find solidity and depth,
And a pumping heart.
Alice returns an angry glance,
Inappropriate to her.
I turn and laugh and look askance,
And quietly concur:
She never shouts or shakes the world,
Or screams, or hurls
At nothing bricks;
She clings to her ideas,
As insects cling to sticks.

Loser's Lament

O kill me, kill me,
Unwanted me.
I want to stay,
I want to flee.
I want to take,
I want to give.
I'd love to die,
But need to live.

One and One is Two

Enjoy your job, but do not rob,
admit to scandal, cause sensation,
move below or above your station,
(Assume a shape),
What matters little matters much,
This is life, it is as such,
You're free to look, but do not touch.

This much I understand
but as for you,
I say you don't add up,
I cannot sum you up.
Do you divide in two?
A silly thought I picked up off the floor.
No, that's not true, I'd put it by the door
to dazzle you when you came in the room,
with head inclined, prepared to find
it empty as before …

I've other thoughts I find in corners dim.
One thought is this, that when you're gone
wars will still be fought and won,
fought and lost,
wooden beams shall still be cut by saws,
washing up will still be done in sinks,
and screams shall still escape from certain doors.
But behind this door you'll hear only laughter,
or cleaning in the spring,
or me preparing conversation to surprise you
when at my door you ring.

But that's no matter, really.
When we picture how things happen
they never happen in that way at all.
I suppose that's why, as you never call,
you'll hear, from behind my door,
a scream or two escaping after all.

Doppelganger

A conical mountain erupts
With lava which splashes about.
My friends would rather the fountain
Of humour I usually spout.

But I must really find the time to laugh,
For still they exhume in this horrible room,
Where drunkards drink out of the bath,
Forgotten old offences,
And build deliberate fences,
Which help secure their station
(Oh, no, there's no relation!).
'Thankyou, Jill,' I'm obliged to say
To one such friend from down Toorak way
Since she empties from a pot
Cooling water on my hot
Dishevelled form.

It's time to fit the norm.

My friends in haste escape the scene,
With parting words conveyed in mime,
And wish me to assume the shape
Which normal men take all the time.

You Don't Know this Man

The man who cast the magic broke the spell.

You don't know this man,
This man walked a tightrope,
This man fell.

The man who saw the shadow saw it well.

You don't know his pain,
A pain eating at hope,
Pain like hell.

The man who saw the sun rise with it fell

You don't take his steps.
His legs, like compass ends,
Turn in circles.

The man who shouldered heaven shouldered hell.

You don't walk his steeps,
Sheer cliffs and elbow bends.
Life in cycles.

Idle Speculation

Have we more movement than the trees?
They're moved by rain, heat and the breeze.
Is wind to trees like others to us?
Do others' actions our own freeze?
Until we figure their reaction
Then bend, providing ease?

Roundelay of Thought

That many men have thought her theirs,
A dream complete, with all its wares,
Has not persuaded *her* to stay,
For the world decides her own way.

And that communism did but detain
The capitalism in its train,
Has gone to show there's nought deters
The world; the path is strictly hers.

A Title Longer Than the Poem

Why
Try.

Justified Love

I love a little snail,
Especially when it's squashed.
And I love a just rebellion,
But only when it's quashed.

And I love a faded picture,
And I love a wasted limb,
But I love a loving better,
And a god without a whim.

Gariwerd

I love these angled rocks.
Yes, Gariwerd, Gariwerd,
What colours seen, what chirpings heard.
In green and greyish shocks;

In fringes frilled, refined;
In trees and shrubs and wood.
Yes, here the poets brood.
And here, a creek defined

By boulder, bank and shrub,
Flows out, out, out
As one expressing clout
To me, the merest grub.

Oh, it's hard to understand

Nature, whose senses command
Inclusion in her joy
For me, an oldish boy,
Who loves her painting hand.

O what a silly art
Is mine, drawing, when this
Creek occludes me in bliss,
Flowing through mind and heart.

My artwork should ensnare
Its viewer's five senses!
Yet it recompenses
Not its tired maker's care.

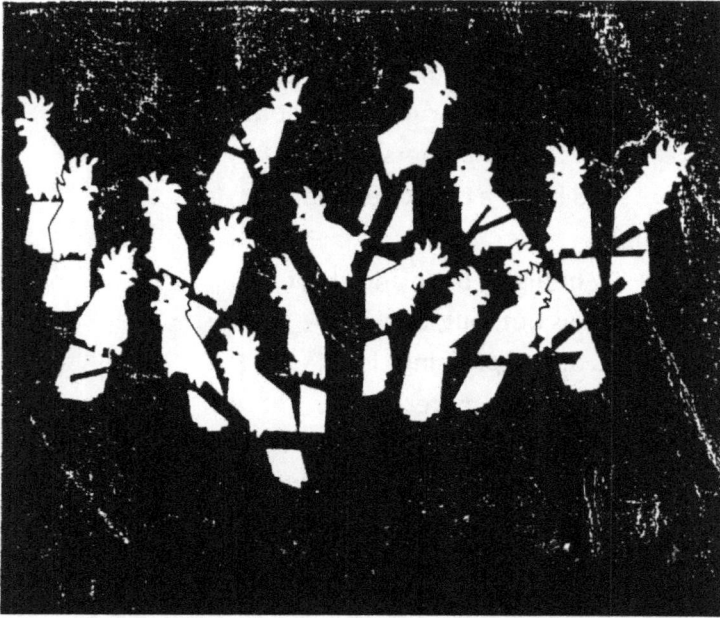

Nature's art evolves through time;
Mine struggles to its feet,
In seconds, vapid, fleet,
Before its couches lime.

Yes, I think I'll go retire,
Why not? Yes, why indeed?
Before I go to seed,
And fumble in faith's mire.

And what if, you say,
What if called upon
To take my pen and don
A cape and come this way?

Well, if asked to create
This wonder, Gariwerd,
I'd close my eyes, turn away,
Pretend I hadn't heard.

Modern Poetry

The crime
Of Rhyme.

MORTALITY

Transientness

Evanescence

Dissolution

Release

Death

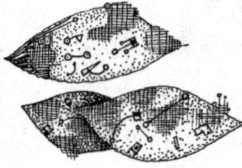

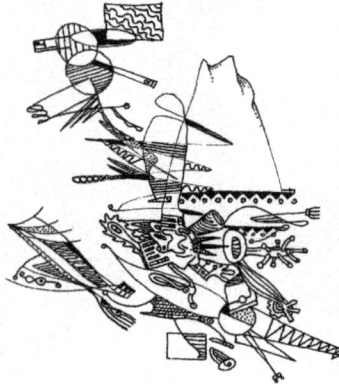

Fisherman's Casket

Where are fish if not in water? With ease,
They're diving gently into mouths (their own
Of hooks now free), and are masticated
In fluid gulps to swim unlighted seas.

Leaving Home

The stick's form belies a crumpled scroll,
And now the papery, crinkly bole,
Its former home,
Is less one family member: fifth cousin on
Its daughter's niece's husband's side, who's gone.
Gone where? To roam
Around betwixt the jaws
Of an animal mostly on all fours.

The Time and Place

When the stars are in their zenith,
   Or the sun is in the sky,
When people are joyous and happy,
   That's when I want to die.

Arrested Development

From a bud to a flower,
   From a seed to a tree,
Only to be cut in this hour,
   And never more be.

Can it Last?

I wander, my vocation,
   A novel in hand;
Frantic gasps of elation
   Are but pinpricks in sand,

That waves seal in memory tombs.

Deities in Spring

I went out late at night, there finding one
I knew, and stopped him, crying, 'Eliot!
'You, whom I read in adolescent years,
'I see have planted in my garden God.'

With automatic snarl and twisted eye
Did Eliot reply,

'O keep the atheist far hence.
'He'll jump the cemetery fence
'And with his nails he'll dig up God,
'You soulless, unbelieving sod.'

I said, 'That's how life always goes.
'You did not know gods decompose?
'Where sniffs a pedigree bloodhound,
'Dear Eliot, rest in the ground.'

This Affliction Thought

The other night I dreamt a dream,
More real than dreams should ever seem,
In which I was a child again,
And my mum was as she was then.
She took me to the city where,
In a green park in the sun's glare,
We chanced upon a seat and saw
A gentleman – oh God, what for?
For Mum – she pointed out the man,
Saying, ah such words, words began
With, 'See that bloke whom I'm espying –
'With wrinkled skin? – he's dying, dying.
'Don't laugh, my dear, I'd fain be lying,
'But why, my dear! you're crying, crying …'

This Is the Way the World Is

Nothing lasts forever,
  All things decay and rust,
And what you could not find in the heavens
  You often find in the dust.

An Epitaph

Now that my coffin's burst its tacks,
  That I am dead, killed unawares,
Please, who is watching through the cracks
  The things I do alone, or cares?

Vast Formless Things

My wooden roof has touched my crown.
Earth above me falls around me,
Countless worms at once surround me.
I am, at last, all gobbled down.

The Dead Are Many

Please, would you shut the lid? I know it's best.
See, the light is keeping me from rest.
Remember now – and stop your shaking! –
That sleep is marred by dreams and waking.

A Message To the As Yet Unborn

You, you that read my written word,
You, you that have my secrets heard,
Know this, voyeur, who doth thrive,
That I was once, as you, alive.

Hear This

World, were you ended when I'm gone
What joy! but you'll go on and on.

Mortality Rate

How many a rhyme
Has been of time?
A lot, and justifiably so,
For we all inevitably go.

Premature Burial

Dead now –
the world's forgot!
yet life
still? ... Time to rot.

Intimations Of Mortality

When I first learnt of death
I paid more heed to breath,
And screamed at Father, as if charmed,
'Dad! why so still? so calm?
'Soon you'll lay full-length embalmed!'

Don't children have a certain charm?

The Watermark

She's dead, John, she's dead, John, and never more will be.
She's gone, John, she's nought, John, that must be plain to see.
But how, John, yes now, John, it's time you ought to know.
So listen, John, and ramble on, but don't you think to go.

Now she was always a quiet and lonely lass,
   Yet she took with a terrible crowd,
Whose leaders were schoolgirls, not more than fifteen,
   But who had all their classmates cowed.

And in their rooms that smelt of pressed flowers,
   Of jasmine, and filigree, and Donne,
One night they stayed up when Sister was soused,
   Telling stories for hours and hours.

They whispered of Wights, and of Witches, and Ghouls,
  While around them the manor house slept,
And the bright chintz, and the firelight,
  Were all of the company they kept.

They picked upon your sweetheart, John,
  In her lace-trimmed dressing gown,
And Mabel smiled, but it was not of the mood
  Of smiles you had courted and won.

They dared her to enter the Newbury Cemetery,
  And hunt out the tomb of young Tom;
And they wrapped her shoulders in a fleecy Madeira
  Shawl for the prowling to come.

'We dare you, we dare you,' they chorused together,
  And not one noted the look in her eye.
It was a look that betrayed she was frightened,
  And held an unanswerable fear she might die.

'Go to the grave where he's lain these past weeks,'
  The leader of the girls huskily ordered.
'It's in the shadow of the church, away from the rest,
  'Under lichen, and by ivy bordered.

'And once you're there, on his dirt-cheap mound,
  'Lift up a pitchfork and plunge it in.'
And they poured her a parting vermouth in a cup,
  Which her hands eventually found.

So she climbed out the window and down the pipe,
  That had so often led to you, John,
But now it descended, like a fire pole,
  To arms more tight than strong.

For it was the night which held her now,
  As tightly as she held the fork.
And all her liaisons with Tom,
  Were busily at work –

Busily remaking themselves,
  In her cold and clamoured mind;
In the wind and in the workings
  Of a ghost, unwept, unkind: –

Young Tom, who had come in the morning,
  While the morning dewdrops gemmed
The pale blade of the verdant green
  And her gown, so neatly hemmed.

Young Tom, who had handed the letter
  So delicately watermarked
With a multi-foliate rose,
  Bled from a passionate heart.

Oh how, thought Mabel, he had flung that heart!
  And how, as assuredly, she would fling it back;
And how, with his death, she had wished to start
  All over – and wring it back.

Yet here she was on an errant dare,
  With the trees in rows like soldiers;
And their branches, stripped and bare,
  Reached out to pinch her shoulders.

Through a dark and winding shrubbery,
  Past villas new and old,
To an iron-gate at the cemetery,
  She stumbled in the cold;

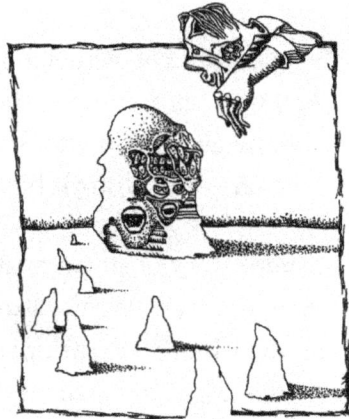

And saw stunted cypresses and aucubus,
   And walls of impenetrable black,
While the pasty white of tombstones
   Crawled like leeches in her sight.

And she found young Tom, and she crossed her breast,
   And with calf-like movements, she raised the fork,
But in plunging it down it caught up her dress,
   And she cried in a manner berserk.

For she mistook the pull for a hand,
   As she had mistaken the lad for a fool,
And the touch of the wind was nothing
   If not indelicate and cool.

Thus, fainting upon the earth, her breath condensed to a cloud,
   The mist about her face was both mantilla and a shroud;
And the cold, the frigid air, quietly caught up her heart,
   And slowly stopped it from beating, and as slowly tore it apart.

And now two gravestones lie,
   Ill-defined, disordered.
They're in the shadow of the church, away from the rest,
   Under lichen, and by ivy bordered.

She's dead, John, she's nought, John, that much you must forgive.
Yes, she's gone, John, she's gone on, and never will you give,
And never more receive, and never will you lie
With her, John, no never, John, she's forever gone.

FANCY

Predilection

Attachment

Gallantry

Fervour

Love

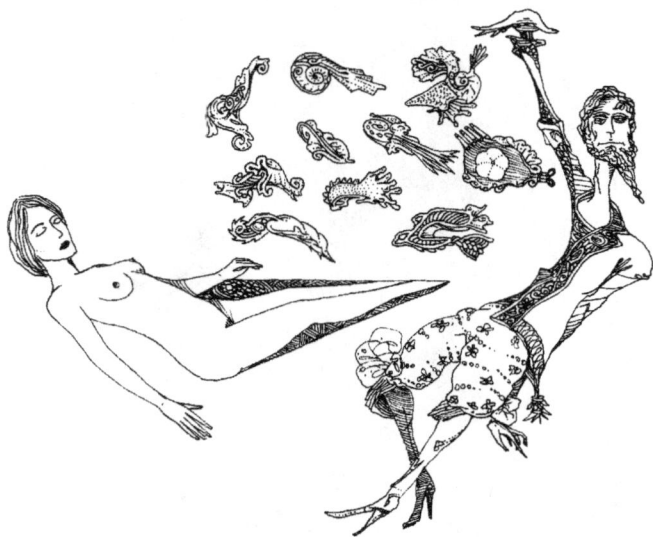

10-Line Élan

Take of this,
Take of that,
Draw of bliss,
Steal a hat,
Wear a smock,
Run amuck,
But do not harm,
Nor wreck nor charm,
But gather me
Within your arm.

Measuring Up

Her calibrated eyes conclude,
'He's tall, yes, good, but handsome nude?
'These two features – one good, one bad –
'Delete each other, all he had.'

What A Shame

We should have parted in the room
  Where we first met.
A friendship that would never bloom
  Was ours, and yet
Just how is one to know by sight
That a person isn't 'right'?

Short Little Love Poem

I worry when you catch the bus
That it might crash, and end us thus.

That Great Evil

If my mind was a box
I would give it to you,
Unwrapped, without
Deception. No secret
Compartments – everything.
It would be my gift.

This gift (dappled with small
Offensive blotches, though
Mostly beautiful) is open to me,
If I let it, so why then
Do I need you to share it?
And why can't I give?
And would you receive?

A World Of Sensible Things

One day in May my friend and I, incurious
About the world of sensible things, imbibed
Each other's thoughts then made thereafter to caress,
But though the wind's a peculiarly distant thing,
Less distant than the mind which moves the hand to touch,
We saw it playing in the grass, and then ourselves.

The Fool's Ditty

I'll tell you what,
  That I'm as me as you are you,
And that, together,
  We make two.

Prayer

When my love holds my hand I pray
That it holds fast, and there will stay.

The Times

What left
Have we to say?
Not much
And still I stay.

So Good

if you could fall in love with me
t'would be
you see
so good for me
and maybe also good for you
I hope that's true,
be good for you.

if I could see what you have seen,
what you have seen and been and heard,
could smell a thought,
could taste a word,
t'would recompense
for every sense
deprived of thee,
t'would be
you see
so good for me
so good for me
so good.

The Convenience

We are
Friends when we meet
And far
Apart alone.

Sleeping Beauty

I met you on a cold and loveless night,
The moon had somehow withered, and the sea had taken fright,
Crashing upon the pier. And there, lying amid the platted coral,
Was you, a slumbering beauty partially hid,

But not so well as to escape my view.
So I tapped my sword upon your casket,
And I kissed your pickled lips, and I touched
Your fetta skin, and I held your salted hips.

But nothing could arouse you, could raise your heavy breast.
'Oh, darling, oh what life we had, there's time for that, for rest.'
And that, it seems, aroused response, in trebles, palsied, seer;
One horrible, horrible cry: 'Oh lover, come not near!'

I screamed, I fell, your demon yell awoke in me desire.
I feinted, parried, rushed in and tarried,
Fell back, enduring, made a thrust,
And watched in horror, watched in fear, watched the rising gust;

And even so, and even then, there came that horrible cry again:
'Oh lover, come not near!' And such is how I found you,
On a cold and loveless night, the moon had somehow withered,
And the sea had taken fright, crashing upon the pier.

Between Head and Heart

Ah, what life, what lips, what laughter!
The head goes first, the heels they follow after.

Love Complete?

They say to be contented with yourself,
Love who you are, for you're the most important,
What others think or feel, stack on the shelf,
Trust your own judgement, be that pain absorbent.
But I say, we can't love ourselves that much,
The marriage is arranged, and then too shortly.
We need another's love, another's touch.
Try to hug yourself – we're none so portly.
That is, we're none so portly to believe
Ourselves a pair. You can't surprise yourself –
The talk's anticipated, despite stealth –
Then, in turning away, both stay and leave.
   Thus though my own self I may love complete
   Without your love 'tis bitter more than sweet.

No Repeats

Once, just once, no repeats,
   You and I, together,
But we didn't put bums onto seats,
   And now it's aired, over – forever.

Oh, *I* was the favourite girl,
   Just destined for fame and for honour,
And you an aspiring dissembler;
   And *neither* a prima donna.

Yes, I remember your short-cropped hair
  (Mine was a natural disaster),
And how we'd run for the number six,
  Breath coming faster and faster;

And how we'd retire, each alone, in the evenings,
  Each alone in their respective pursuit:
Me, glazing yellow on ochre,
  You, rehearsing that old King Canute.

But England was so far away!
  And scumbles took so long to dry!
And then, in a wink, it was day.
  Oh, well, it won't rectify ...

But why did you not pick me flowers?
  Yes, flowers – with a root attached.
And why did I sleep all those hours,
  When minutes I should have snatched?

Why? Yes, why did I slumber those nights,
  Rugged-up in those blankets I bought?
The cold was never outside. Besides,
  What was the worst I could have caught?

By God we were stupid people,
  And now the days coalesce into this:
Your hand upon my hand one time,
  And one platonic kiss.

Alright, you gave me a flower once,
  But it didn't come in a batch.
So, what is one to do with a rose?
  It's pretty, but where's the catch?

GRAVITY

Despondency

Melancholy

Joylessness

Vapours

Sadness

Nursery Rhyme

Mummy, do you think that the monster will take me?
Mum, would you hear me if I were to scream?
  For the night is so dark,
  And the bed it is tall.
  Upon four wooded legs –
  What is under them all?

Mummy, I *asked* you to come in and wake me.
I've gone and slept right through my dream.
  Please, the night is so dark
  That you can't see at all;
  Whether the monster's in bed,
  Or there – on the wall!

Mum, please, I've *got* to be standing, so shake me.
Quick! 'fore the monster can play out its scheme!
  Help, the night is so dark,
  As it comes down the hall,
  Its horn out for skewering,
  Its fingers to maul.

But the sleeper wakes to nightmare,
And the nightmare never sleeps.

Mum, you knew that the monster would take me.
Mum, you hear every time that I scream.
  Now with night so dark,
  Like a funeral pall,
  I get into bed,
  Turn to the wall.

Cassy

The other night I dreamt a dream,
  And lest it end I swam, agleam,
Amid its swirling torrents to the past,
  Where Cassy, buried dog of mine,
Again was living, looking fine,
  And as she was when I beheld her last,
With brilliant coat of black and white
  The black of night, the white of light,
As if the two collided in her making;
  But Day had thought my dream to wade,
To slash it with its scalloped blade,
  Then silently to kill it dead in waking.

The Self

These eyes, unheeded beacons, flash!
The globe is gone, the message trash.

Susanna Wren

Susanna Wren lives in a house
Of padded concrete, has no spouse,
Is sixty-two, and ends each day
When 'washed' and 'wiped' and 'put away.'

Queries of the Moon

How shall I shake the very world?
  Where shall I build a shelter in it?
And how are bricks at life I've hurled,
  Evidence of me within it?

Pointing the Finger

Who do I blame for ...?
What do I blame for ...?
For ... – for everything!
For all that is bad,
Melancholy and sad?
For that which darkens
Dull and pallid dreams
Gone rife?
Myself, for its
Continuation
In life.

An Exercise in Misanthropy

Swamped in horrid human waste,
  Far away in time and place,
Lives man in his confuséd haste,
  A nasty, undeserving race.

Mirror Mirror, On the Wall

I look upon a mirror on a wall,
And see myself as ugly, after all,
Yet turn as if from heat expelled by fire,
And with these words condemn myself a liar,
'No, that's not me, whose eyes my eyeballs chase,
'And that is not my voice, nor that my face.
'No, that's not me, reflected in the glass.
'Let what may come, but do not let that pass.'
  I looked upon a mirror and I saw,
  Not everything as changed, but as before.

The Namers name me ugly and I am.
The Namers name me things *ad nauseam*,
Ascribing attributes, which I've then got.
I declare myself a beauty, but I'm not.
They ask me if I'm this or if I'm that.
Would I prefer the perfume or the hat?
Ha! let Miss Snow White be as white as snow;
I'll wear my hair long like some cacti grow.
  Again what did I see? Well, men, I saw
  That everything was changed, and as before.

Slugabed

Rarely will the world dance, dance in my front door.
Mostly it sleeps upon its back (so as not to snore),
Or, when awake, it's out with friends, friends it won't ignore.

I Know Not What

Something is wrong, I know not what.
If wrong in me, uncovered be!
Something is sad, there's sadness in me.
So what is wrong? I know not what.

The Pigpen of Men

O Missus Mavus,
Come quickly, save us!
Bring us back from the pigpen of men
To the small little den
Of a childhood now gone.

Yes, Missus Mavus,
Please hurry, save us,
From the unending unhappiness,
And the unstoppable rapidness
Of growth.

But, Missus Mavus,
I'd have you save us
Only I expect
Your lilting frame
Of life's been wrung
For you were old
When I was young.

Questions to an Older Me

When I was young I often shed tears.
  Were they
Unwarranted tears or prescient fears?
  Useless useless tears.

When I was young, alone in my bed,
  I feared
My parents would die, alone I would cry.
  Were *they*
Unwarranted tears or prescient fears?
  Dumb, unnumbered years.

Robomen

I am in a dark ravine,
Where glints on quartzite rock are robomen,
Agitating at my spleen.

Now I'm atop a broken stump,
Beneath which, in chasms deep, a fen
Bears gigantic toads that jump

To this world to eat its men.
Do such diversions make *you* wonder why
Actual fiends must kill and die?

Unlimited Extension

I rather think we talk to God
   When no one else will listen,
Or when we simply want to kill,
   But think we're on a mission.

Cardboard Cut-out People

I see some cardboard cut-out people so away I run.
I wish I had some transport, and I wish I had a gun.
These cardboard cut-out people, cut so neatly into shape,
(The shape of one generic man, unfolding hand in hand),
Come chasing me, oh chasing me, forever will I race
up here, careen up there, oh why, oh why, and when and where?
Their sides are shallow, yet their cuts are deep, but never more
will I retreat, nor stoop to countermand.
But please, God, when will they disband?

Good on you, Gertrude

Good on you, Gertrude, Good on you, Gertrude,
Good on you, Stein.
Gertrude Stein, no friend of mine.

Give over sequential story-telling;
Modernism take a seat.
Give over punctuation and spelling;
Modernism take a seat.

No, not functionalism,
Not functionalist architecture,
No, I cannot dislike the Catholic, his beads;
The executive, her tie; the ruler, its markings;
As I get off on the ionic column, its fluting.
I get off on
I get off on
What of syntax?

After all your tom-foolery, you modernists,
your obscurantism, the *Wasteland*,
which oh so confused –
after all this, what now?

Good on you, Gertrude, good on you, Gertrude,
Good on you, Stein.

Oh no, I so need it, this detail.
Oh no, I so want it, some meaning.
Abstract art; don't give it me.
Nothing will come of nothing, nothing will.
I cannot become conversant with the artist's meaning.
What's she saying, or he, what?

Unlike life, its antithesis, death,
Is nothingness with*out* embellishment.

Give me.

Oh repetition's so fun, fun, fun it's so
fun repetition. Repeat endlessly my days

Say something different, say it.
Anything different, say it.

Oh no, don't get me wrong, Mondrian, I, too,
like things pared away to their essentials, but
but   but
but without my upper class bearing, my
school boy tie, equations to compute, my
artistic interests, what then?
Oh no, give me, give it me.

Good on you, Gertrude, Good on you, Gertrude,
Good on you, Stein.
Good on you, Gertrude, Good on you, Gertrude,
Good on you, Stein.
Gertrude Stein, no friend of mine.
She's evil and she's quite unkind,
She's Gertrude, Gertrude Stein.

Gertrude Stein in her underwear
is not unlike a grisly bear!

Say something different, say it
Anything different, say it!

Like Lambton's Worm

Beneath a greying, somnolent sky,
Where clouds are puffed and porous pillows,
  There lie
A field of lonely trees, with drowsy leaves that droop, a-weary,
Shot from twigs like trills atune to some clairvoyant air,
  Told upon the wind.

And where I hide, in a starless
Stygian starkness, does the world
  Decry
My ambling dog-trot, jog-trot, slow-coach, foot-pace, acrawl
For nothing could quicken me, or hope to once ensnare
  My moonless mind.

No, not mad, not me, no soul entombed, preservéd dead.
  No fear, you see I sit beside
  A stream of thoughts, unbidden, wide,
    Inside my head;
  Beside a stream beholding thoughts
    Unread.

No, fine, I'm feeling fine. Please, understand it's me.
  My hand entraps such drowning thoughts,
  Ah, such thoughts, such feelings wrought
    From liquid reverie;
  Hearkening to a world of lock
    And lea.

See how my hand ensnares a thought?
  Marring the progress of others?
And how another thought is caught!
  What was the old it smothers?

What thought? That slithers from the bow!
Oh God, I see it now!
It's the thought that takes the form
Of a fat and blooded worm,

Which scratches, latches
Onto my body, burnt by matches.

I feel it kill me, will me
With energy dead.
Its breath of onion
Smarts my head.

In shape, what does this thing confirm?
Articulated like a worm,
But with scales, spikes, and painted fangs,
It feeds on guilt and mortal pangs.

Yet can I flee or quietly stray?
For no, the mind's aware,
   By the hunger, by the wear,
God, the mind, unruly, knows,
   By the iron, as it glows,
   With the torture, with the flare,
That the worm's about to close.

Yet can I turn or run away?
No, the mind, it fully feels,
   By the slicing, by the weals,
God, the mind appreciates,
   By the serpent, how it hates,
   That cut up, the skin but seals,
To a stronger form and fate.

Yes, the worm has come
And the worm is great.

But that it would come, I guess I knew.
Whilst skirted in my thoughts, it grew.
And though I've sliced it through and through,
The many bits have fused anew.
It grows! Dear God this worm will me undo.

WHIMSY

Ridiculousness

Doggerel

Humour

Madcap

Reverie

The Philosophy Pharmaceutical

Empirical evidence
has never made any sense
for us, the Bombley Wimbley Nombley Jice.
A priori truths suffice.

Now Sue's a sumptuous friend of mine,
my auntie, and a woman too,
who lives in Woomallaloomallaloo,
where a green snake is not green,
and unhidden things remain unseen.
But each long night she asks herself,
When stacked upon the topmost shelf,

'Could one have failed to lead to two?
'Could earth have been a giant loo?
'And did existence *really* need to be
'a composite of work and tea?

'O why? o why?'

This is how the answer goes,
'No one knows, no one knows.'

Bag-of-bones

There was a man who loved to eat,
  himself he loved to eat,
and only on himself would sup,
  in the style of men effete.
He ate and ate and ate and ate,
  from head to flaccid feet.
Upon his flesh he dined so well
  he ate up all his meat.
'I'm bred,' he said, 'so that my meat
  '(so rarefied and sweet),
'is all I condescend to eat,
  'since none its stature beat.'
He spoke no more; I felt he was
  A body incomplete.
This man of whom I speak I add,
  to sympathy entreat,
he may be but a thing of bone,
  yet praise his noble feat.

Ben

His thoughts are of dinner, our Ben,
Yet his thinking ascends now and then
To the vaguely astute,
And sharply acute,
But mostly it centres on 'When?'

The World as Will and Idea

On a hilltop, by a city,
In a castle, dark and pretty,
Lives a maiden, fair and witty,
But she's HEADLESS!

                       … What a pity.

Afternoon Of an Ant

Hark, we never know how the world sits.
  Come, stare into this sugar bowl,
  Watch the cascading sugar dune,
  And remark, as it buries ants,
  How others traverse its sliding slants.
Can we ever know how the world sits?

Amenity

I love my little toilet,
I love it through and through,
I love its porcelain make,
I love its well of blue.

What the Black Forest Cake said
to the Lemon Meringue Pie

Sometimes I wish to eat you but I don't.
  You might not taste so good.
Sometimes I wish that you would nibble me,
  But fear that it might hurt.
Besides, our tastes are different.

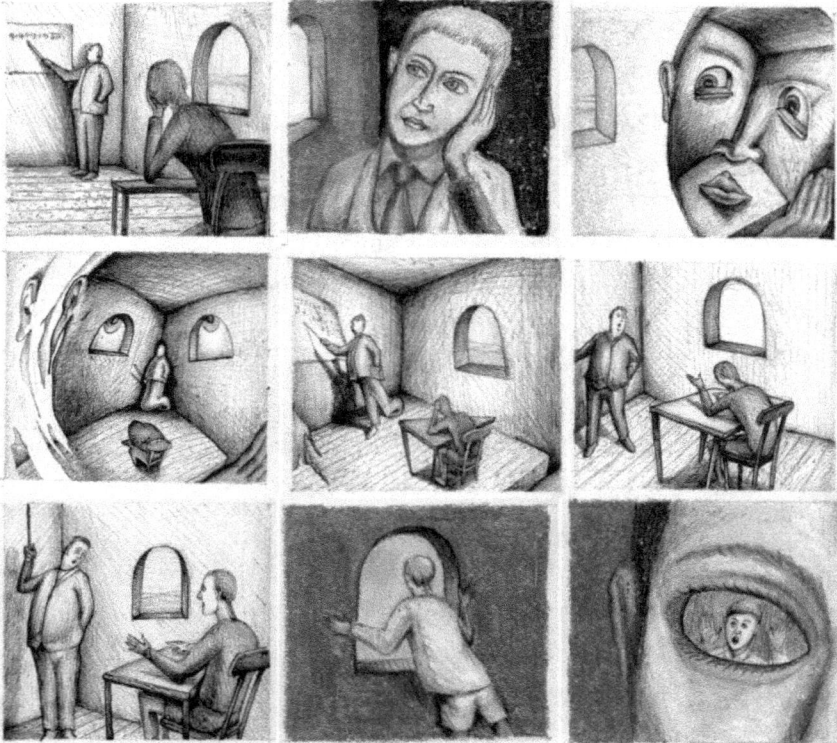

Captive Sun

The sun sat on my windowsill.
   I rose, it rose, and we met in the sky.
The sun sits on my window still
   Because I keep it level with my eye.

The Muse

My muse is away today,
My muse is away.
Away today, today away,
But she's left me out a tray.

Daylight Horror

The sun! will it never
But poorly dissever
The Shadow from its nooke?
The Bunyip from its brooke?

Dexterity Comes Quick

Blunt fingers caked on a spoon
Can but hold it too soon!

Banners Glorious, Golden

I, a dripping drunkard, hung out
on the line, hung out to dry, am
drip-drop drying, drying in the wind.

Along the Ramparts

Mum hangs the ghosts upon
the line. Tonight we will
wear them, and haunt our dreams.

I'm in Another World, Your World's in Mine

I'm in another world, your world's in mine.
I'm feeling stupid, you're feeling fine.
Oh well, whatever, never mind.
Oh well, whatever, what's the time?

That's it, my sanity's just given out on me.
Can't be mended, here it's ended.
There's a song in the air but the fair Senorita,
Fa la la, do re me, don't leave the teabag in the tea.

'Oh, alright,' she said, 'I'll bring in the paper and buy the bread,
'But just you try and mend that head.'
'I'm sorry, dear, of course, I swear,
'But this is why, and *please* do try,
'The tannin leaks right out of it, and leaves it tasting worse than shit.

Impotent Omnipotence

God is mercy,
God is love,
Missiles are falling from above.

Royal Slander

The British Queen erupts in tears
  At every chance she can,
Because, you see, her youngest son
  Has never played the man,

The man, the man, the man, the man,
  The man, the man, the man,
The man, the man, the man, the man,
  The man, the man, the man.

'Now Edward, dear, you're slightly queer,'
  She said to him in Surrey.
'I charge that to the Windsor Ear,
  'Which always was a worry,

'A worry, worry, worry, worry,
  'That Windsor Ear's a worry,
'A worry, worry, worry, worry,
  'Please marry well and hurry!'

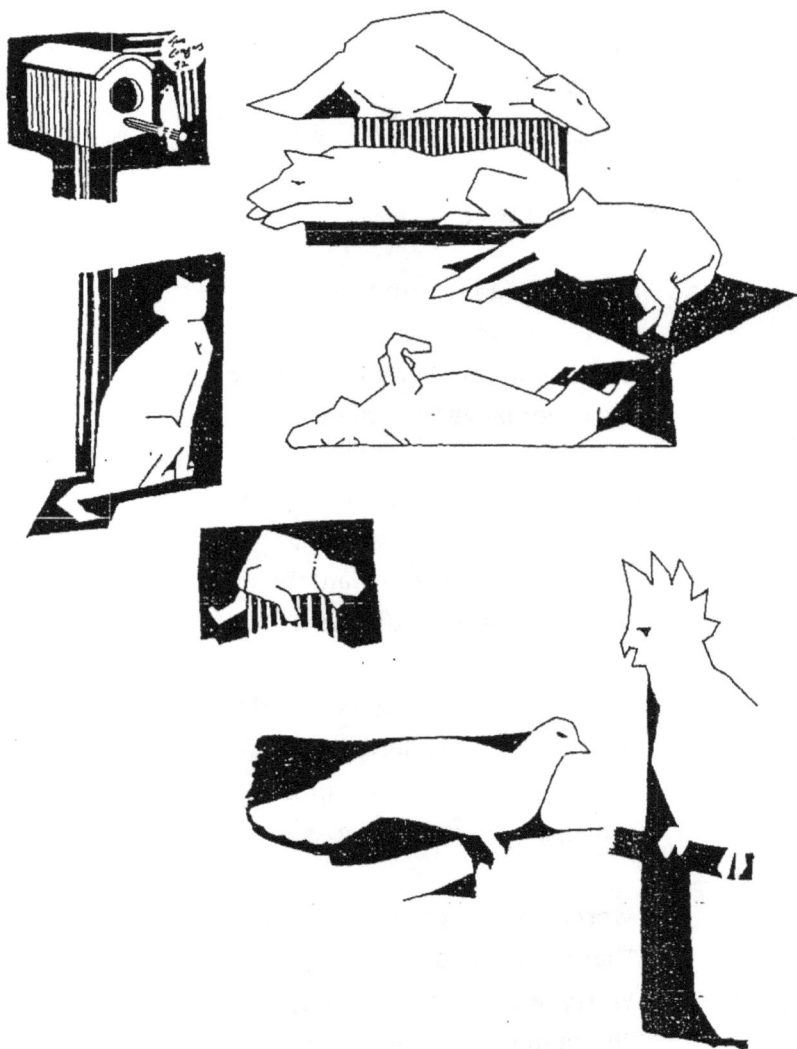

[As Evening Vomits into Dawn]

As evening vomits into dawn.

The Mentalist

The cat, a reclining nude,
   Cleans his paws upon his mat.
A dog, the usurping brute,
   Roughly removes his friend, the cat.

With one considerable swipe,
   The cat's thrown in the air.
The dog proclaims the fire,
   And stretches there.

But played out in his mind,
   In images most vivid,
The cat beats the dog,
   Until the hound is livid.

Life Story

Another day
Wanked away.

One & Twenty

(with apologies to Samuel Johnson)

Long-expected one and twenty
Years have past – how time has flown!
Pain and pleasure, pricks and princes,
Dear Miss Clarke, are all your own.

Childhood now is all but over.
Adulthood has taken sway.
Still you can, by make-believing,
Happy be and childish stay.

For all who pause to ponder, query,
Smart to see the world in pain:
Here the prankster sunny, leery;
There the thinker swamped with rain.

So here's a cynic's line to follow:
Don't expect and don't believe.
All but you are false and hollow,
Clean your plate, and nothing leave.

Take the old, forget the newer,
Value friends who keep tight-lipped,
Be as open as a sewer,
Caution no-one, take a dip.

Flowers, fungi, frangipani,
Bastards, claimants, carts that tip,
Fry & Laurie, Pa and Granny,
Once unpleasant, now are hip.

And when you're forty-two remember,
Half of that is twenty-one;
And that which is finished sooner,
Is earlier begun.

So if your mother or your father
Tells you off for wilful waste,
Scorn the counsel, and their odour,
You can stink or wash at last.

Hamlet

For a play about performing,
Polonius had no tact,
Ophelia was a 'nearly-a',
And Hamlet couldn't act.

The Promise

I *know* I talk in italics,
I know I laugh in rhymes,
I know I die daily,
But fewer and fewer times.

And I know I wear in places,
But there is something I won't do;
Your advice is ever with me:
Don't fade right through.

PROSPECT

Perspective

Habitation

Landscape

Abode

Realm

Melbourne My Beloved

You, me, in Melbourne Drive-Through romance,
Under blankets with Surround Sound,
Golden Arches bobbing in a slow dance,
Form a Dolby Stereo mound.

You're my Virtual, hip, Morphine-Drip —
You're the one;
My Multimedia Encyclopaedia
Optus Vision Optimum.

Melbourne, some say you've gone commercial
But for an infomercial
On the pleasures of a city by the sea,
That's fine by me.

The View from the Rialto

I see a scene of pillared halls,
  With ceilings in the skies,
And crowds congealed below with walls
  Reflected in their eyes.

The Trees Arthritic

By night the bush is beaten black and blue,
The moon relieves this flatness with a ghostly, silvery hue,
The trees, arthritic, stretch and creak,
The wind exhales between.
What picture have I painted?
What can it mean?

Murrumboola

In winter Nature's joy,
  But now it's summer time
  The creeks all choke on slime.
O world how you annoy!

No! slime combats *my* creek,
  And wins and overfills
  The water where it spills.
And now, no more, can speak;

Its mouths are dried and damned.
  Look, a lazing snake uncurls
  Its coils in rhythmic twirls
To sip some mud on hand.

Some mud?! Unquenched it leaves.
  Ah, awful, awful thirst.
  I feel its soul's accursed.
On through the grass it weaves.

But my eyes have in their scopes
   Still drier visions like
   A crack-line in a spike
Of rock that skyward gropes.

A spider in this crack
   With web ensnares a fly,
   A fly now soon to die,
A fly stung in the back.

But meantime how it swings!
   Within its private gibbet,
   Whose silken bars inhibit
All movement of the wings.

It is a silk-wrapped
   Parcel of food.
'Ugh!' – How typically human,
   Yet decidedly rude!

The Plank

Today
A plank fell on the sunning grass
That, yellow with fright, will now pass
Away.

The Wall

Between all things a wall stands in repose.
And rarely has this wall been known to fall,
For, built up, red brick by red brick, and thick,
Row upon row, a stretcher bond for strength,
And reinforcing rods along its length;
Few things can bring it down, if things at all.

  And even then, nothing holds out for long
  Because the wall is wide as it is strong.

No, nothing staves off its mad force,
For the concrete's cured with short, unsettled hose,
Turning from green to white, as leaves leach light,
Urging the root to straighten in its course.
Oh, inclement anger *is* in splashes spent,
But splashes of green, with trunks infirm and bent.

  Surely from birth it's built, each brick a year or tear,
  The mortar, sand to grit the eye, the lime to leach and wear.

Yes, between all things this wall stands in dispute,
Dividing cities, house from house, and house from street;
The cattle from the sheep, the cows from bulls on heat;
The ache from its desire, the act from good repute;
Imperfect gestures from their fine reception;
And children from the world, as from deception.

  Yes, between all things a wall stands in repose,
  Except between a life and that life's close.

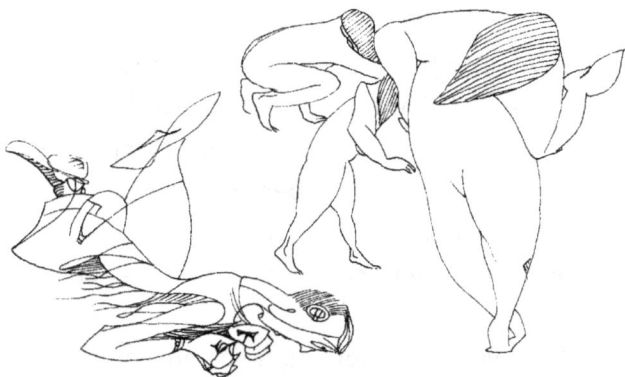

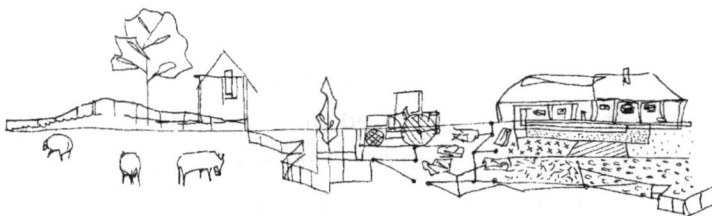

On the Farm

On a paddock on a farm,
  Adjoining those with wheat,
The randy rams attend the sheep,
  The firstling lambs they bleat.

These sheep, like tufted clouds
  Snagged upon the bladed grass,
Are interrupted when,
  Coming through the pass,

A farmer and his dog
  Herd them to the shed,
And there some throats are cut,
  And there some fleeces shed.

Slaughterer slaughtering,
  Life unliving,
The taking's easier
  Than the giving.

On the paddock on the farm,
  Adjoining those with wheat,
The weaning lambs in silence mill,
  The ewes are processed meat.

Continental Plates

Two continental plates
  In a monumental rift
Decide to pitch their weights
  In a continental shift.

These monumental foes,
  Having once collided, take
To piling mountains high,
  Which one day they will break.

The Gum Tree

Poor old gum tree, whose bark's been rent,
The things which made your bark their tent
Have gone, your roots are in soiled earth,
And concrete clutches round your girth.

Patchwork Plain

Threadbare clouds unravel yet
  Their silken swaths of rain
Till, perforce, they then beget
  A crazy, quilted plain.

Ennui

This jaded city wakes today,
Forgetting yesterday and may
Forget today.

Thought in traction.

Street smells ferment in wearisome heat,
The world stirs, revolves – but sleeps.

Alas, inaction.

Arising from your bed, this morn,
With eyes upon this lazing dawn,
Your senses warn
Of what the day will bring to you.

But first a guide:

He is smiling with you,
wherever you go.
Meet your mind, say hello.
Hello. An answer! – You have a friend.
Just one?

Yes, just one, but one will do
To while away an hour or two
On the boardwalk by the strand,
While this lazy city looks so busy,
But is nothing quite so grand.

A short retraction:

This city - did I say it *wakes* today?
Yes. Oh no, it never wakes.
It aches, aches, aches.

Melbourne

It's dawn; your car begins to take
  The bends with just a hint of brake,
Whilst people wake from salted slumber,
  And dreams they cannot number.

Can you see it? Heark,
  A brown, almost a reddish, spark,
A match newly lit?
  Here, on Sydney Road,

And there, in the city outskirts,
  Going oh so fast?
What is in the rear view mirror
  Is done with, already past.

But watch, it edges, like a time-lapse
  Film – the day, I mean,
  In jump-cuts unsmooth, unclean,
And now it's noon, or two perhaps,

And your car has travelled to where
  Verticals bring relief.
The loneliness, the emptiness,
  How time was spent and brief.

But getting on, getting on,
  We come to late afternoon
And so does it –your car, its sheen,
  Once glistening brown, now dried maroon.

And in the mid-life sun the world assumes,
  In tints of brazen gold,
A likeness to a Pharaoh's tomb,
  Unutterably old.

And still it hurtles forth!
  And others are overtaken.
Some by so close a margin
  They're left distressed and shaken.

Now within – what quivers there?
  What shape? what creature writhes about?
Perhaps we cannot know,
  But we know what goes without,

  For passing by,
Projected on the glass,
  Are visages of things that were
And quickly come to pass.

But heedless to such,
  Your car goes on.
Oh ever on, anon, anon,
  Top gear, no need for clutch.

Yes, on and on whilst the scenery blurs
  Into one single shot:
An image of the sights recalled,
  And those remembered not.

Then, with night approaching soon,
  The traffic lights come on.
They indicate the road ahead,
  Behind, the road that's gone.

When dark, these orange lights become,
  As viewed through squinted eyes,
The colour and effect of rum
  That beckons to the rise.

Once topping this, your car goes down
  Into a darkened valley,
Where a bridge spans across a creek
  Fringed by the river malley.

And you won't remember tomorrow,
For you have already forgotten today,
And your children will reflect with sorrow
On the day you drove away.

The End.

www.ingramcontent.com/pod-product-compliance
Lightning Source LLC
Chambersburg PA
CBHW020550030426
42337CB00013B/1029